Gardening

Organic Gardens

Lori Kinstad Pupeza
ABDO Publishing Company

visit us at
www.abdopub.com

Published by ABDO Publishing Company, 4940 Viking Drive, Edina, Minnesota 55435.
Copyright © 2002 by Abdo Consulting Group, Inc. International copyrights reserved in
all countries. No part of this book may be reproduced in any form without written
permission from the publisher.
Printed in the United States.

Photo credits: Corbis, Corel
Contributing editors: Bob Italia, Tamara L. Britton, Kate A. Furlong, Kristin Van Cleaf
Book design and graphics: Neil Klinepier

Library of Congress Cataloging-in-Publication Data

Pupeza, Lori Kinstad.
    Organic gardens / Lori Kinstad Pupeza.
        p. cm. -- (Gardening)
    Summary: Describes how to make an organic garden.
    ISBN 1-57765-748-9
    1. Organic gardening--Juvenile literature. [1. Organic gardening.
2. Gardening.] I. Title.

SB453.5. P86   2002
635'.0484--dc21   2001043620

Dial Before You Dig
Before digging in your yard with a motorized tiller, call your local utility
company to determine the location of underground utility lines.

Contents

Organic Gardens

Planting an **organic** garden is good for the environment. Organic gardeners do not use chemicals. They use natural materials to **fertilize** their plants and keep pests away. This keeps the organic garden from poisoning the environment and upsetting the natural balance between **ecosystems**.

People, plants, and animals live in ecosystems. They are dependent on one another for food and shelter. Ecosystems are affected by how we use soil and water to grow plants and flowers.

Organic gardening ensures a safe environment for people, plants, and animals. Organic gardens exist in harmony with nature, and are safe for all living things.

*It is possible to grow an abundant crop of
great-tasting food without using chemicals.*

Getting Started

To begin your garden, you will need some gardening tools. One handy tool to have is a small hand shovel called a trowel. It is useful for planting your seeds and **seedlings**. A rake or hoe will also make preparing the soil and removing weeds easier.

When your garden is first planted, you will need tools for watering. A watering can is good for watering small gardens. A bigger garden will need a sprinkler and a garden hose with a sprayer.

Later, after your garden is established, it will get most of the water it needs naturally, from the rain.

Gardening Tools

Turning Soil & Weeding

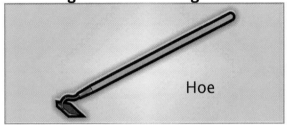

Hoe

Raking

Garden Rake

Watering

Watering Can

Hose

Planting

Trowel

Digging

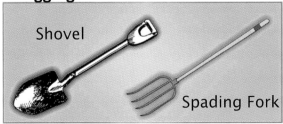

Shovel

Spading Fork

Pest Control

Sprayer

Where to Plant

Once you have your tools, you will need to decide where to plant your **organic** garden. Look around your yard. Make note of where the buildings and trees are. Notice where the soil drains well, and where the low areas are that drain poorly.

Also pay attention to things such as bodies of water or large, shady trees. These can create **microclimates** in your yard. Try to locate your garden in an area with consistent temperatures.

You will need to work in your garden every day, so locate it where you can easily get to it. Also choose a plot of land that isn't too big. Even small gardens can be a lot of work.

*An open, sunny area near your house is
a great place to plant a garden.*

9

Garden Soil

When planning an **organic** garden, it is important to know what kind of soil is in your yard. There are four different kinds of soil. They are clay, sandy, humus, and loam. To find out which type of soil you have, dig up a little and take a handful. Squeeze it into a ball.

Clay soil will form a hard lump and stick together. If it's wet, it will feel sticky. Sandy soil won't stay in a ball shape. It will slip through your fingers. Humus soil is made of **decomposed** organic material and will stick in a ball. Loam is a balanced mixture of clay, silt, and sand.

When you go to an organic garden center to pick out plants, look at the tags on the plants. They will tell you whether the plant will grow in the type of soil you have.

Good soil is an important part of a garden's success.

Preparing the Soil

Learning about the soil in your yard will help you grow a better garden. Since an **organic** garden is chemical-free, the soil will be important to its success.

After you have determined what type of soil you have, you will need to determine its **pH** level. You can buy a test kit at a garden center. You can also call your state university's extension service. Often, your extension service will test your soil free of charge. It can also recommend soil testing companies in your area.

To adjust pH, you will need to add **nutrients** to your garden soil. Lime or limestone will raise the pH. Sulfur will lower it.

Always work with an adult when treating your soil's pH. You will need to wear a mask, gloves, a long-sleeved shirt, and long pants. Wear socks, and shoes that completely cover your feet.

It will take a few months for your soil's **pH** level to adjust. So, you may want to begin preparing your garden's soil a season in advance.

Testing soil in a cornfield

Making Plans

Now it's time to plan the layout of your garden. To begin, get a piece of paper, some markers or crayons, and a book about **organic** gardening. Then, make a map of what you want your garden to look like.

Start with a small area. A three foot by five foot (1 m by 2 m) garden will be big enough to begin with. Remember that you will have to weed and water a lot when your garden is beginning to grow. So, even a small garden can be a lot of work.

Draw the outline of your garden on the paper. Color in where you want to grow each plant or flower. Keep in mind how much space each plant will require as it grows bigger. You will also want to arrange your plants so that the taller plants will not shade the shorter plants from the sun.

A well-planned garden

Seeds

Once you have planned your garden, you can start planting. Before you begin planting, check the frost **zone** map to make sure the possibility of frost has passed in your area.

To plant seeds, read the directions on the seed packets. Then make a trench with your hand or trowel. Drop the seeds in and cover them with a light layer of soil. Don't plant them too deep. Seeds need to be watered every day so that they will **germinate**.

Growing a garden from seeds can take awhile. You might want your garden to grow faster. Or perhaps you cannot find seeds for all of the plants and flowers you want to grow. In these situations, you may want to plant **seedlings**.

Seed packets have useful information on how to plant, water, and grow the seeds.

COSMOS

These early-blooming, daisy-like flowers will bloom until frost.

Plant Height	Plant Spacing	Planting Depth	Days to Germination
3-4 ft.	12-15 in.	1/4 in.	5-10

PLANTING INSTRUCTIONS
Plant in sunny location. Cosmos will grow in poor soil.

When to Plant Outdoors

	May-June
	April-June
	March-June
	Jan.-June
	Jan.-Dec.

16

Frost Zones

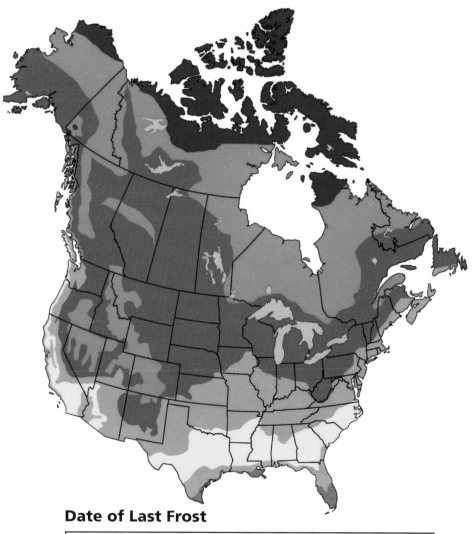

Date of Last Frost

February 1		June 1	
March 1		July 1	
April 1		August 1	
May 1			

Seedlings

If you buy **seedlings**, you can have an instant garden. An **organic** gardening center will have a wide selection of organic seedlings.

To plant a seedling in your garden, first dig a hole slightly bigger than the seedling's roots. Then pull the plant out of its pot by gently holding the plant upside down and tapping the bottom of the pot. Put the seedling in the hole. The base of its stem should be even with the top of the soil.

Fill the hole around the seedling with soil so the seedling is snug in its new home. Press firmly around the base of the plant and water it. Over the next few days, give it lots of water.

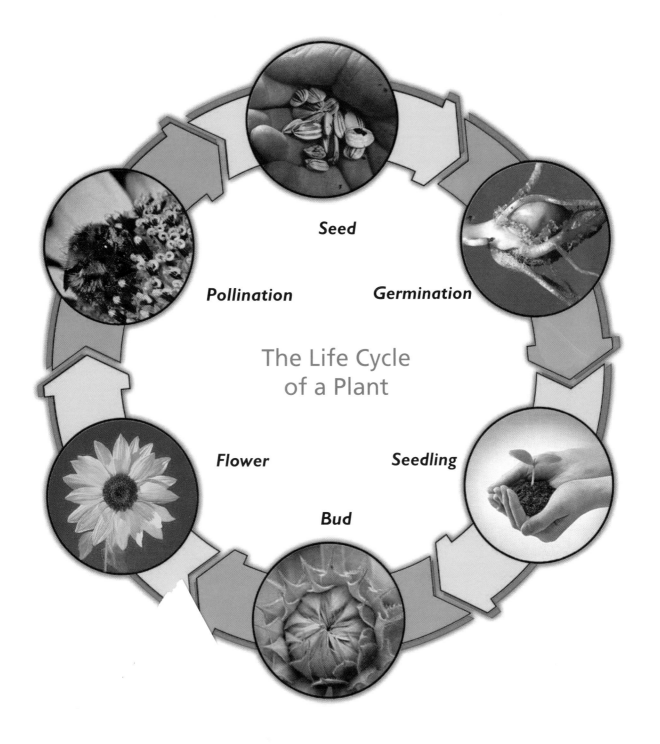

Seed

Germination

Pollination

The Life Cycle of a Plant

Flower

Seedling

Bud

Watering

When you first plant seeds and **seedlings** they will need to be watered almost every day. As your plants grow, check them daily to see if they need water. Are they drooping? Are the plant's leaves turning brown? This means the plant needs water.

Watering often with a sprinkler will make the roots dig deeper for water. Deep roots will make the plants stronger.

Watering your **organic** garden will make your plants grow well. Unfortunately, any weeds in your garden will also benefit from the water. Weeds will compete with your plants for water and **nutrients**. So, you will need to keep the weeds out of your garden.

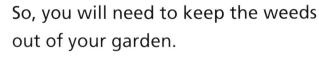

20

Don't forget to water your plants.

Garden Care

Weeding is an important part of caring for your garden. It's a good idea to pull weeds out by their bases. This makes it easier to pull up all their roots. Eventually, your plants will grow bigger. Then there won't be room in your garden for weeds to grow.

To prevent weed seeds from **germinating** in your garden, spread mulch between your plants. Mulch also keeps the sun from drying out the topsoil. Some gardeners spread hay or grass clippings between their plants. Rocks and wood chips also work well.

Watching for animals and insects is another part of garden care. If animals are eating your plants, you may need to put up a fence. Bugs also like to eat plants. If you see spots or holes on your plants' leaves or stems, you will need some kind of pest control. **Organic** gardeners use earth-friendly pest control methods.

This plant has been mulched with gravel.

Organic Pest Control

Growing an **organic** garden means you don't use chemicals to control pests. If pests are eating your plants you can use organic methods to control them. Many ingredients needed for organic pest control can be found in your home.

To control ants and other insects, mix one tablespoon of liquid detergent with one gallon (4 L) of water. Spray the mixture on your garden. This should keep the insects away from your plants.

Vinegar is also an excellent organic **pesticide**. Fill a bowl with vinegar and cover it with lettuce leaves. Place it in your garden. Vinegar works especially well if you have problems with snails or slugs.

Another method to control insects is to spread wheat flour mixed with cayenne pepper around the plant's base.

Controlling pests in your **organic** garden is important for healthy plants. But be careful not to kill all of the insects in your garden. A good balance keeps the soil healthy.

Organic gardeners discourage garden pests in an earth-friendly way.

Companion Planting

Many gardeners believe that some plants do well when planted near each other. They also believe some plants should not be planted together because they hinder each other's growth. Choosing plants that benefit from each other is called companion planting.

Companion planting also helps **organic** gardeners control pests. When certain plants are planted near each other, they keep away unwanted insects. Others create an environment that welcomes helpful insects. Still others help each other grow by providing shade or sharing **nutrients**.

There are many companion plant groupings. Plant corn with cucumbers, pumpkins, or squash. Plant tomatoes with onions, carrots, or parsley. Plant lettuce with carrots, radishes, or cucumbers.

Just as some companion plantings promote growth, some plants do not grow well near each other. Do not plant potatoes or dill with your tomatoes. Keep tomatoes and corn separate. And if you want to grow healthy peas, plant them away from onions and garlic!

Pumpkins grow well with corn. The corn stalks shade the delicate pumpkin vines from the harsh sun.

A Fun Project

Compost bins

Compost is a great **organic fertilizer**. Compost is made of air, water, and alternating layers of brown and green organic materials. You can buy compost at your garden center or nursery. But it's also possible to make your own compost.

To start a compost pile, you will need a compost bin. You can make your own or buy one from your garden center. Place the bin in an out-of-the-way location, but near your garden.

The first layer of brown material

Add kitchen scraps to your compost bin. Do not add meat scraps or animal fats.

To make the compost, first spread a layer of brown leaves or pine needles on the bottom of the bin. Next, spread a layer of grass clippings or kitchen scraps on top of the brown layer.

Keep alternating layers of brown and green until the bin is full.

Then add dirt or compost, and enough water to moisten the compost pile. Last, turn the compost occasionally to mix it up. Soon you will have dark, healthy humus to **fertilize** your **organic** garden.

Finished compost

Glossary

decompose - to break down into simpler compounds.

ecosystem - a community of organisms and their environment.

fertilizer - a substance used to help plants grow.

germinate - to sprout and begin to grow.

microclimate - the climate of a small site or habitat within a larger climate or habitat.

nutrients - vitamins and minerals that all living things need to survive.

organic - plants grown using natural fertilizer instead of chemical fertilizer.

pesticide - a substance used to destroy harmful plants and animals.

pH - a measure of soil's acidity or alkalinity. It is measured on a scale between 0 and 14. Acid soil has a pH between 0 and 7. Alkaline soil has a pH between 7 and 14. Soil with a pH between 6 and 7 is neutral. Most plants like neutral soil.

seedling - a young plant grown from seed and not yet transplanted.

zone - one of five climate-derived divisions of the United States. The U.S. Department of Agriculture created the zone map based on each zone's average low temperature.

Web Sites

Aggie Horticulture
http://aggie-horticulture.tamu.edu/kindergarden/kinder.htm
This informative site from Texas A&M University has a great composting slide show, information on nutrition, and suggestions for getting children involved with plants.

Gardener's Supply Company
http://www.gardeners.com/gardening/bgbpest.asp
Read about organic pest control, how to identify garden pests, and how to prevent them.

These sites are subject to change. Go to your favorite search engine and type in Organic Gardens for more sites.

Index